ALSO BY PAUL MULDOON

Frolic and Detour

Frolic and Detour

FARRAR STRAUS GIROUX / NEW YORK

Paul Muldoon

Farrar, Straus and Giroux

120 Broadway, New York 10271

Printed in the United States of America

Originally published in 2019 by Faber & Faber Limited, Great Britain

Published in the United States by Farrar, Straus and Giroux

First American edition, 2019

Library of Congress Cataloging-in-Publication Data

Names: Muldoon, Paul, author.

Title: Frolic and detour / Paul Muldoon.

Description: First American edition. | New York : Farrar, Straus and Giroux, 2019.

Identifiers: LCCN 2019020217 | ISBN 9780374158392 (hardcover)

Classification: LCC PR6063.U367 A6 2019 | DDC 821/.914—dc23

LC record available at https://lccn.loc.gov/2019020217

Designed by Crisis

Our books may be purchased in bulk for promotional, educational,
or business use. Please contact your local bookseller or the Macmillan
Corporate and Premium Sales Department at 1-800-221-7945, extension
5442, or by e-mail at MacmillanSpecialMarkets@macmillan.com.

www.fsgbooks.com

www.twitter.com/fsgbooks

www.facebook.com/fsgbooks

10 9 8 7 6 5 4 3 2 1

FOR JEAN, CONSTANTLY

Contents

Frolic and Detour

The Great Horse of the World

The first thing I remember is being stepped on by a horse
while it paused to stale,
paying me no more heed
than it would an upset pail
of water or feed
or a comb dragged through the coarse
hair of its mane and tail.

The great horse of the world stamps and champs at the bit
and lays back one ear
as I approach
from the rear
to hitch it to the world-coach,
mindful of keeping at least one hand on it
so it knows I'm still here.

Encheiresin Naturae

If Jupiter and Saturn meet,
What a crop of mummy wheat!
—W. B. Yeats

When farmers purchase a patented seed variety, they sign an
agreement that they will not save and replant seeds produced
from the seed they buy from us.
—Monsanto

1

Not for the first time would we wrest the heavy door
of the barn from its jambs.
The door had been painted the red of iron ore,
the posts daubed with the blood of a lamb

to protect us from the Angel of Death.
It all had to do with two interpenetrating cones.
One of the pillars of the sons of Seth
was built of brick, the other of dressed stone.

No wonder almost everything did pass over us—
passed us over or by—
wealth, fame, true love. For now we would astound

ourselves with a pig hanging from a roof truss
as if it might be making a half-hearted attempt to fly
before falling hard to the ground.

2

Whatever it was that fell there on the ground
cheered us as manna had cheered
the Israelites. It might have been a little mound
of lime where someone who volunteered

for sentry duty made his mark
even as a sniper found his. The stench of bristle-singe
is the stench of battle. Up at Coole Park
everything had seemed to hinge

on Ted Burke from the forge in Gort
and the particular angle
of a particular piece of steel. These Landrace boars

had been known to give a snort
of disdain as they broke free of the brangle
and ventured out so high above the threshing floor.

3

The cries of a chorus of women on the threshing floor
arose from the wide-skirted stooks
of corn milling about. As if they were party to a score
being settled. Settled by hook or by crook

over winter ditching and hedging. Tom Trout
and Michael Minnow
at loggerheads. The boar sticking its snout
in the air to reprimand those presuming to winnow

the wheat from the chaff.
Tom Trout insisting on Charles Stewart Parnell
having been the uncrowned

King of Ireland. A salmon on its gaff
forced at last to draw the line. A salmon's death knell
going back to its having overstepped the bounds.

4

We flailed away at wheat sheaves that were bound
with straw ropes and stacked
against the future. Sometimes one hound
would break free of the pack

and singlehandedly raise the hare
while the rest looked on, torn
between a sense of Duty and the Devil May Care.
It seemed no time since the corn

had been silk-fine and green.
Now a hare was couched in the last square of barley
to be mown. No scythesman was a match

for its mobility any more than a woman who gleaned
the field was fit to parley
with the blue tit, the bullfinch, or the nuthatch.

5

The pikestaff that had been hidden under the thatch
since the United Irishmen made their stab
at freeing the country wasn't a patch
on the Viking halberd. The Vikings loved a slab

of bacon as much as the next man,
so much so that every Irish sow and her farrow
lived in dread. The Vikings liked to fan
the flames between Peter Plough and Harry Harrow

while riding roughshod
over both. Their hauberks were almost as close-knit
as their families. Peter Plough was known to wring

out a greasy sod
in the selfsame sodden pit
from which a mud-walled cabin would shortly spring.

6

Our two-roomed cabins were thrown up in the spring
in a matter of days. No dressed stone. No brick.
Nothing more complex than coming to sling
mud at the straw ricks

in the farmyard. They say King James
was a victim of the very scurf
for which he had the cure, making a right hames
of the idea of the Royal Touch. A dust of turf

rising from the bog
had our eyes itch. When we weren't tortured
by midges there was always the chance we'd catch

a finger or thumb in the cog
of a mill wheel or machine. Deep in an orchard
Patrick Pike was limbering up for a butcher-batch.

7

Since the Royal Irish Regiment had been dispatched
from India to France for the Sturm und Drang
of battle, the wind lifting the latch
on a half-door had sent a pang

through a chimney breast.
A Clydesdale mare at the smithy
might have put her best
foot forward. Tom Trout might have bent a withie

in two to mend a turf- or salmon-creel.
There was often a sweep
like this when the spirit of the corn took wing

from the last sheaf. It seems revealed religion reveals
that as you sow so shall you reap,
be it in the agricultural sense or the romantic fling.

8

What we thought had been the noise of the flurry-fling
of hailstones was, in fact, a hail
of bullets while the King's
laying on of hands against whatever might ail

a body was a hen's yarn.
That there might be something beyond the crypt
or bounty in the barn
were ideas that outstripped

all others. Despite the pact
between us, God's advances
were mostly unwelcome. Once we relied on a hoard

of seed that had been sacked
and saved. Once we took such chances
as that ample-bosomed door still seemed to afford.

9

Last spring an apple-blossomed door might still afford
the opportunity to make a better fist
of managing the farm. The drains might be shored
up by men as yet unwilling to enlist

in the British Army. Now it was all pig-singe stench.
Now there was no healing potion, no philter,
for Minnow, Michael, or Trout, Tom, in their trench.
It used to be things would seem out of kilter

only when a Clydesdale mare
was taken lame
from having stepped on a harrow pin

or a farm boy was somehow denied his share
of true love, wealth, or fame—
whatever a farm boy might have the chance to win.

10

Now a farm boy had barely the chance to win
a crop of hay. Only if the rain held
off for the rest of June. The scar on Tom Trout's shin
came from that time a felled

tree fell on him. Ted Burke had deemed it a breach
in nature when weekend guests at Coole Park
carved their initials into a copper beech
and did its bark

a major hurt. Coole. The Irish word for "hazel." *Coll.*
A hazel rod was used by a diviner
to find not only wellsprings but nine kegs

of brandy buried at Gort. We were all in the pull
of the moon, even in Asia Minor,
the moon being merely the stamp of God's wooden leg.

11

When a forked hazel rod began to shake a leg
it was a sign that something stirred,
be it Leda's third egg
or the suspicion those sepoys wouldn't be deterred

much longer by cartridges greased
with pork fat. This was an era when pig killers,
postmistresses, and priests
were widely perceived as pillars

of society in whom the sum
of knowledge to which we might ever want to appeal
was still safely stored.

I, meanwhile, had developed a rule of thumb
whereby almost everything had to do with a deal
struck between that famous poet and his spirit board.

12

The famous poet would commonly use his Ouija board
to conjure spirits where they threshed
upon the threshold of this world. This underscored
his theory that a spirit will mesh

with this world of slime
as readily as, in Egypt,
mulch bonded with muck. Not for the first time
had the bravest souls shipped

out with their provisions for a long march.
Take, for example, the 1st Battalion
of the Rifles. A drum was often made from horseskin.

The rainbow arch
in its neck meant the mane of a stallion
was prized above all for stringing the bow of a violin.

13

There was scarcely need to string the violin
given how the hedgerows throbbed
with the unholy din
of blue tits and bullfinches. The doorposts were daubed

with blood. I suppose that, at dusk,
a cartouche might look somewhat like a cartridge.
The poet's talk of cones or souls waiting for new husks
went right over our heads like a partridge

taking off over the barn before once more falling hard.
Now we had found ourselves in a realm
of frog storms, clegs,

the cart in the yard no longer the cart in the yard
but an Egyptian chariot fashioned of willow and elm
and held together by ash pegs.

14

The steam-bent wild fig felloes fixed with willow pegs
dated the cart in the Middle Kingdom. It would convey
a king to the other side, along with his nest egg
of gold, hawks, combs, beer, a ration of wheat per day

forevermore. What a wind whispered in the corn's ear
back when it was green and silk-fine
had now been made abundantly clear
as the harvest was gathered in. Now we could resign

ourselves to a horse-drawn mowing machine
having come to the end of its cycle.
One funnel had poured

into another. Given the choice between
it and the fates of Trout, Tom, and Minnow, Michael,
not for the first time would we take the door.

15

Not for the first time would we take the heavy door
off the barn and lay it out on the ground
so it might double as a threshing floor,
then flail away at wheat sheaves we had bound

only a month before. The straw would thatch
our mud-walled cabins the following spring,
the wheat make good its promise of a batch
of bread for a wake- or wedding-fling.

Tonight this besomed door might still afford
a slack-jowled farm boy the chance to win
one of the girls who'd shown, and shaken, their legs

and danced their hearts out on its sounding board.
Now Ted Burke dusted off his violin
and, one by one, tightened the tuning pegs.

Memphis

To set all four paws on an upturned tub
and not topple over was as much as I could manage
even when I still strode into battle with my lord Ramses.
Mite-ridden then, raw with mange,

I became a mascot for Amenhotep,
no less integral to his ménage
than any of the menagerie lounging on the ramps.
The sawdust-stuffed baboons were known to munch

on peaches by the bushel, so their urine
was notably high in cyanide.
After a last ration of beer flavored with aniseed

I was set down between a giraffe and a rhino.
My face was recasting itself from the one I'd been assigned
to the face of a pharaoh from the Fourth Dynasty.

2

My face was the face on the royal sarcophagus
I'd guarded for many an age, my haunch the lion-haunch
of the sun-god, Sekhmet.
All I had to go on was the hunch

that if I could but focus
on the task I might eventually will the hinge
of my knee to move. I'd already consulted the schemata
of the necropolis so was able to inch

past the pyramids,
then make my way through thorn forests,
the arid patches, grassy plains . . .

Now I've followed those trademark red triangles on beer mats
to a sawdust ring where nightly I'm forced
to set all four paws on an upturned tub and hold my balance.

Pablo Picasso: *Bottle of Bass and Glass* (1914)

Dante Alighieri drank it straight no chaser.
Even though he talked in circles he never stood his round.
Anonymous drank with "fowles in the frith."
Giovanni Boccaccio drank with Geoffrey Chaucer.
Mulled wine. Nutmeg. Lemon rind.
William Shakespeare drank with Master Froth.
Emily Dickinson drank from her saucer.

Bradstreet and Berryman were known to imbibe.
Dean Swift drank before delivering a homily
though Daniel Defoe avoided whiskey like the plague.
Martinus Scriblerus drank with Alexander Pope.
John Milton drank with Edna St. Vincent Millay.
God had a drink or two with William Blake.
It was mostly with Wordsworth Coleridge liked to tope.

Christina Rossetti more than once paid homage
to Alfred, Lord Tennyson's
having more than once crossed the bar.
W. B. Yeats drank with some guy called Selwyn Image.
Ezra Pound was somewhat into Zen.
Delmore Schwartz drank with a heavy bear.
Louis MacNeice drank with the Ulster scrimmage.

Oliver Goldsmith drank with a deserted villager.
Mary Shelley drank with Leigh Hunt.
Robert Frost drank Scotch over ice.
When T. S. Eliot drank with Valerie Fletcher
she wasn't taking shorthand.
Marianne Moore drank through a snake-scaled hose.
Dylan Thomas drank on his stretcher.

La Rochefoucauld drank with Madame de Sévigné
which is why he contracted gout.
W. H. Auden drank with Harold Norse.
Igor Stravinsky drank with Warren Zevon.
Having lain so long by the Gateless Gate,
Thomas Merton drank with his nurse.
Raymond Carver may have drunk to get even

with the likes of Gordon Lish.
R. L. Stevenson drank with J. M. Barrie.
Joseph Brodsky preferred potato vodka to wheat.
Malaria's not an issue for the G & T lush
while a second lemon rind will stave off beriberi.
I myself drank wine, both red and white,
though I always drew the line at blush,

having been brought up in a world where fusel
oil was part and parcel of every batch,

a world in which push almost always came to shove.
Elizabeth Bishop drank with Alice Methfessel.
Patrick Kavanagh drank with that McDaid's hodgepodge.
Robert Lowell drank aftershave.
You could say we all drank from the same vessel.

Georges Braque: *Still Life*
with Bottle of Bass (1914)

Dante Alighieri drank it straight no chaser.
Even though he talked in circles he never stood his round.
Anonymous drank with "fowles in the frith."
Giovanni Boccaccio drank with Geoffrey Chaucer.
Mulled wine. Nutmeg. Lemon rind.
William Shakespeare drank with Master Froth.
Emily Dickinson drank from her saucer.

Bradstreet and Berryman were known to imbibe.
Dean Swift drank before delivering a homily
though Daniel Defoe avoided whiskey like the plague.
Martinus Scriblerus drank with Alexander Pope.
John Milton drank with Edna St. Vincent Millay.
God had a drink or two with William Blake.
It was mostly with Wordsworth Coleridge liked to tope.

Christina Rossetti more than once paid homage
to Alfred, Lord Tennyson's
having more than once crossed the bar.
W. B. Yeats drank with some guy called Selwyn Image.
Ezra Pound was somewhat into Zen.
Delmore Schwartz drank with a heavy bear.
Louis MacNeice drank with the Ulster scrimmage.

Oliver Goldsmith drank with a deserted villager.
Mary Shelley drank with Leigh Hunt.
Robert Frost drank Scotch over ice.
When T. S. Eliot drank with Valerie Fletcher
she wasn't taking shorthand.
Marianne Moore drank through a snake-scaled hose.
Dylan Thomas drank on his stretcher.

La Rochefoucauld drank with Madame de Sévigné
which is why he contracted gout.
W. H. Auden drank with Harold Norse.
Igor Stravinsky drank with Warren Zevon.
Having lain so long by the Gateless Gate,
Thomas Merton drank with his nurse.
Raymond Carver may have drunk to get even

with the likes of Gordon Lish.
R. L. Stevenson drank with J. M. Barrie.
Joseph Brodsky preferred potato vodka to wheat.
Malaria's not an issue for the G & T lush
while a second lemon rind will stave off beriberi.
I myself drank wine, both red and white,
though I always drew the line at blush,

having been brought up in a world where fusel
oil was part and parcel of every batch,

a world in which push almost always came to shove.
Elizabeth Bishop drank with Alice Methfessel.
Patrick Kavanagh drank with that McDaid's hodgepodge.
Robert Lowell drank aftershave.
You could say we all drank from the same vessel.

The Leader

I did eventually renounce raspberry picking and rosary camp
for the hotbed
of Belfast, surviving there on black pudding, Bell's, and Badoit.
The life of a BBC impresario

allowed not only for hols in Spain and Portugal
but moonlighting with Osip
Mandelstam and sad-eyed Fernando Pessoa.
At thirty-five I substituted clapboard

for bonny clabber and found myself in the innermost recesses
of the Ivy League. There I boned up
on Wimsatt and Wilmot (*pace* Vivian de Sola Pinto)
in much the way El Cid read Caesar,

hoping to show such legerdemain
whilst laying down a curtain of fire behind a fire curtain.
If ever anyone inquired
about my life as a midlevel manager,

"Terrific," I always said, "Terrific . . ."
The corpse of El Cid
was propped up in his saddle
the better to lead his army towards that one last victory.

In the Field with Mangas Coloradas

For three days I'd kept my eyes fixed on his saddle drape.
Three days since our combined force
of Bedonkohe and Chokonen
had tracked down General Carleton by his fifes
and drums. Maybe because they were volunteer troops
the fighting was uncommonly fierce.
I still see Mangas striding through the canyon
and laying about him with a Sheffield butcher's knife.

What Mangas hadn't allowed for was a pair of howitzers
bringing up the rear. Those fairly took the wind
out of our sails.
Not only was Carleton able to stave
off our attack, we were forced to retreat in disorder.
Though Mangas had suffered a bullet wound
he still held on to his battle-zeal
as we rode to Mexico. "Close shave," he smiled. "Close shave."

On that third day, I had one of those moments of clarity
when fast-forward skitters and skids to slo-mo.
That darkening patch on the saddle-drape.
Now I would perceive
the name Mangas Coloradas
derived not so much from a penchant for red calico
(thrown in for good measure with butcher knives and beaver traps),
but his bloodstained sleeves.

Corncrake and Curlew

The corncrake marvels at the land being green
although the winter's harsh.
The curlew knows the land's so green
because it's mostly marsh

rendered by a few broad strokes
of a palette knife
and the merest whiff of tents, wood smoke,
a red jacket, drums and fifes.

This same corncrake once hitched its star
to a horse-drawn reaper.
The curlew, meanwhile, has ranged so far
it's now been issued with a beeper.

The corncrake ratchets up the odds
of being cut down in the aftermath.
The curlew has followed an execution squad
along this muddy path

to the telephone pole
that's still smeared
with creosote-blood and the bog hole
into which the body's disappeared.

The corncrake sounds but one alarm.
Faithless, fickle,
the curlew moves from big farm to big farm
with its little scythe or sickle

to oversee pig killing, the shearing of sheep,
the combine's thrum and strum.
Its lonesome wheep's
a counterpoint to fife and drum.

The corncrake's oblivious to its rasp
catching a sentry off guard.
The curlew's come to grasp
the idea that running a credit card

across a fine-tooth comb
is a surefire corncrake summons.
From its observation dome
the curlew has long since taken in the comings

and goings of little platoons
filing off three-mast ships
and hauling to lorries parked beyond the dunes
crates of rifles and rifle clips.

The corncrake marvels at the land being green
although the hay's been saved.
The curlew knows the land's so green
because it's a mass grave.

Belfast Hymn

1

"A sandbar near a river mouth"
would give Belfast its name.
The river where we've slaked our drouth
and where we staked our claim

with those who built the Giant's Ring
five thousand years ago,
with Normans, Essex, the Dutch King,
with Chichester & Co.

For even Ptolemy the Greek
set his sights on the Lagan.
He used to come for the Twelfth week
despite warnings of "dragons."

Although we're sometimes seen as staid
we've tossed our bowler hats
and cheered on every new parade
across the tidal flats.

2

The Vikings gave us a wide berth
and focused more on Larne.
They'd overrun the Solway Firth
and ransacked Lindisfarne

so they had nothing left to prove
about their derring-do.
We'd kept the Picts at some remove
despite their being True Blues.

What really put us on the map?
The world viewed through the prism
of eggs and bacon in a bap.
It's a Belfast baptism!

It's seen us through our darkest hours
and salved our troubled souls.
Since we were granted devolved powers
we've all been on a roll.

3

Although we've so much on our plate,
we take it as a badge
of honor to eat twice our weight
in wheaten farls and fadge.

What sets the Ulster Fry apart
is its calorie count.
It's a clear insult to the heart.
The casualties mount

from Portavogie to Ardglass
where they've given up erring
on the side of caution, alas,
determined to prove herrings

and prawns will happily coexist
if served on beds of dulse.
The reason why they hold your wrist?
To check if you've a pulse!

4

For Belfast's long been a byword
for hospitality—
the slice of barm brack, lemon curd,
the drop scones at high tea.

It's for sponge cakes and Sally Lunns
we Belfast people yearn.
A spot of bother? All "wee buns,"
as far as we're concerned.

Most of the things we love to share
are made with cream of tartar
though any putting on of airs
is a complete nonstarter.

It's Adam's ale straight from the tap
that we still most esteem—
unless it's Châteauneuf-du-Pape
or Costières de Nîmes.

5

Although it's true we do enjoy
a pint and a wee Bush
restraint's the technique we employ.
We just don't like to push

unless it's with a certain tact,
like when we're simply forced
to read someone the riot act
for backing the wrong horse

or give our caddies an earful
when we've kicked up a divot
or into a *Titanic* hull
hammer those white-hot rivets . . .

That great ship waiting to be launched
was set off down the slip
by men like us. Stalwart. And staunch.
And taking no auld lip.

6

That smell's the smell of retting flax
from County Down flax dams.
Some sheets are sewn from old flour sacks
but some are monogrammed.

For from the cradle to the grave
we wear our linen bleached.
We see it breaking like a wave
on a North Antrim beach

where some diehards still like to surf
and some fish in chest waders.
We know that artificial turf
is favored by Crusaders

along with polyester mesh.
In times of joy or grief,
of course, there's nothing quite so fresh
as a fresh handkerchief.

7

The Belfast Ropework Company,
the largest in the world,
kept us from being all at sea.
The Queen of the May birled

her leg and hunkered down to caulk
a seam with hanks of goat
hair even as she scanned the lough
for Shorts' new flying boat.

It's known Shorts aircraft had a fin
sometimes described as "ventral."
Known, too, the best of days begin
and end at the Grand Central

where we counter the cold and damp
with oatmeal, ancient grains,
entrecôte aux champignons, champ,
a flute of gold champagne.

8

The flute on which James Galway soared
was really made of gold.
Some dwell in the House of the Lord
and some on the threshold

of hotels like the Maritime,
Van Morrison and Them
summoning from our glow and grime
melodious mayhem.

When Sam and Dave fell foul of Saul
they took refuge in Naioth.
For us there's no escape at all
from Samson and Goliath

except perhaps to lose ourselves
in big band and bebop
as we go thumbing through the shelves
of a used vinyl shop.

9

Those two iconic gantry cranes
have held us in their thrall
long after they've thrown off their chains
or we've had any call

for their great feats of strength
or other shows of force.
History holds us at arm's length
until the Dutch King's horse

charges us from a gable-end
and Henry Joy McCracken
expounds on all that might impend
while on Cavehill the bracken

brings us right back to the Bronze Age
and a cauldron's dull glow.
It's time to check the pressure gauge
in case the whole thing blows.

10

And what we cherish, it would seem,
are the rough and the smooth
of Brillo pads, Brylcreem,
tang, tungsten, tongue and groove,

the sliced pan, the sliced plain, plain fegs,
jaw-box sinks, wheelie-bins,
the goatskin bodhráns, the Lambegs
made from their kith and kin.

When we bake apple tarts or pies
we keep it in the family.
The apple on which we rely
would be an Armagh Bramley,

resistant as it is to scab.
We ourselves resist blabs, blowhards,
gasbags with the gift of the gab
(unless it's our own bards).

11

For though we've lost some afternoons
drinking from a tin can
in the snug Crown Liquor Saloon
beloved of Betjeman

we've also found our poets best
sustain us with their words.
Now we're known less for snipers' nests
than nests of singing birds

we laud the poetical wing
where Mahon, Longley, Hewitt,
McGuckian, and Carson ring
out the seed-bells, suet,

and bacon rind they've set in store
against our winter wants.
We track them still on the foreshore
by their typewriter fonts.

12

Our painters, too, have seen the light
where water meets the sky.
Cadmium red. Titanium white.
How often have they vied

for supremacy in the air?
Andrew Nicholl giving a vague
sense Cavehill might still shelter bears.
Tom Carr, James Humbert Craig,

Dermot Seymour's foot-rot- and fluke-
ridden sheep, William Conor,
Rita Duffy, the great John Luke
whose many selves we honor

as we struggle with points of view
and depth real or perceived.
They come at us out of the blue
where sea-heave meets land-heave.

13

Though the green hills lie on all sides
we come back to red brick.
Short, narrow streets run far and wide
as if they were homesick

for Manchester or Birmingham
and not Dublin or Cork.
In times gone by we'd run ram-stam
with pikestaffs and pitchforks

across those cobble-littered streets
and then put on the kettle.
Long years of beating a retreat
have made us show our mettle

and muse at length upon the stuff
we're made of. Granite. Gault.
We jubilate in being gruff
and gracious to a fault.

14

We like to get down to brass tacks,
the no-frills nuts and bolts,
but not before we've had some crack.
We do tend to revolt

against whatever powers might be.
We rejoice in high jinks,
gooseberry jam, Nambarrie tea,
Irwin's malt bread, Kerr's Pinks.

Some like potatoes "balls of flour"
and some prefer them waxy.
Some hire a limo by the hour
and some hop a black taxi

to visit those old trouble spots
on the Shankill and Falls
before taking one last straight shot
back to the City Hall.

15

For years we found it hard to wean
ourselves off giving vent
to something very much like spleen
against those we resent.

But now we harbor not a grudge
but something more like hope.
Even the hardest heart will budge
when we throw it a rope

unless it fears being pinned down
like that high-profile giant.
That doesn't play in Sailortown.
That makes us more defiant.

We revel in the linen mills
and the yarns they still spin.
Though on all sides lie the green hills
we'll never be hemmed in.

16

For if the future's less than clear
that won't leave us nonplussed.
It's not our style to live in fear
of what's in store for us.

Our shipyard workers packed their gear
and a "piece" in a box.
But now it's peace we've engineered
and christened in the docks.

The spirit of those men of steel,
their gray-eyed wives and daughters,
will keep us on an even keel
through the uncharted waters.

For we steer by the Northern Star.
However far we roam,
that "river mouth near a sandbar"
will signal we've come home.

Walnuts

1

Bringing to mind the hemispheres of the brain in the brainpan,
these walnut halves are as ripe
for pickling now as in 860, the dye in a Viking girl's underdress
then being derived from walnut husks. I hear you stifle
a yawn when I note that steamed
black walnut is generally held to be inferior to kiln-dried
while the term à la mode de Caen
refers specifically to the braising of tripe
in apple cider. I who have been at the mercy of the cider-press
have also been known to trifle
with the affections of a dryad in a sacred grove,
a judge's daughter and a between-maid to Lord Mountbatten
among others from beyond my clan.
It was only as recently as 1824 we first used the term "to snipe."
Walnut was the go-to stock wood for both Brown Bess
and the Lee-Enfield bolt-action, magazine-fed, repeating rifle.
Each has seen service on the shores of Lough Erne
in the hands of both wood-kernes and followers of the First Earl.

2

Our own interpersonal relationships have tended to be so askew
it was only as recently as 1844 we first used the term "scarf"

of the neck-garter. Girding up the loins
for a family feud has often proved the more fecund
line of inquiry. Walnuts are now deemed
good against malignancies of breast and prostate—not only tried
but tried and true. From time to time you
and I have met on a windswept airfield or wharf
where we've seen fit to join
battle without ever having reckoned
on how the Irish law on treasure trove
would change in the light of the Derrynaflan paten,
never mind King Sitric being the son-in-law of King Brian Boru
who prevailed over him at Clontarf
or, at the Boyne,
William of Orange's putting paid to his father-in-law, James II.
It was at the Boyne, you recall, that Ahern
gave Paisley the "peace bowl" turned from a local walnut-burl.

The Ambulance

Surely Leonardo drew up plans
not only for the army tank, the parachute, and the helicopter,
but for the ambulance
in which we still hope to capture

alive a native of East Harlem
or the Holy
Land of East Belfast, carrying him into the realm
of beef tea and green Jell-O

from which so few have returned. It was da Vinci,
after all, who designed a mechanical lion
with a lifelike finish
that prowled the streets of Lyon,

reaching into the cavity
where its heart
might well have ticked and proffering gifts
of lilies to the citizenry . . . Lilies and arrowroot

scent this anteroom
that has come to fetch from a dim
studio off the Antrim
Road or Amsterdam

Avenue another upstart Michelangelo
about to suffer
the indignity of having been duly
summoned by a note he can't quite decipher,

a note from some long since
unmasked spy, some secret admirer,
some sergeant at arms from a world that now makes sense
only in our rearview mirror.

1916: The Eoghan Rua Variations

Do threascair an saol is shéid an ghaoth mar smál.
Alastrann, Caesar, 's an méid sin a bhí 'na bpáirt;
tá an Teamhair 'na féar, is féach an Traoi mar tá,
is na Sasanaigh féin do b'fhéidir go bhfaighidís bás.
—attributed to Eoghan Rua Ó Súilleabháin (1748–1782)

1

On Easter Monday I was still en route
from Drumcondra to the GPO when I overheard a dispute
between a starch-shirt cuckoo
and a meadow pipit, the pipit singing even as it flew
between its perch on a wicker-covered carboy
and the nest it had improvised near a clump of gorse
from strands of linen spun by Henry Joy
and the mane of a stalking horse.
The cuckoo that had shouldered out the hoi polloi
showing not a hint of remorse.
Now the world's been brought low. The wind's heavy with soot.
Alexander and Caesar. All their retinue.
We've seen Tara buried in grass, Troy trampled underfoot.
The English? Their days are numbered, too.

2

Of the nine hundred Mauser rifles Erskine Childers and the
    boys
unloaded from the Asgard in Howth, most were deployed
to the Volunteers. Childers traced "Howth" to its source
in the Old Norse,
the Vikings being among the first to beat their plowshares
into swords. On account of his opposition to it, the headstrong
O'Rahilly was simply not made aware
of the impending ding-dong
even though the blacksmiths on Mountjoy Square
had been going at it hammer and tongs.
The wind blows ash now the world's completely destroyed.
Alexander. Caesar. Each leading a mighty force.
Tara's overgrown. Look at the cut of Troy.
With the English, things may eventually take their course.

3

At Jacob's biscuit factory, Thomas MacDonagh sends up a
    flare
through the arrowroot-scented air.
On Stephen's Green, meanwhile, the English try to wrong-
foot us by launching a two-pronged
attack on our trenches. "The more we're spurned,"

Roger Casement once opined, "the more we're engrossed."
His submarine shaking from stem to stern
as it hugged the Kerry coast.
"The least stone," he went on, "the least stone in a cairn
is entitled to make one boast."
The whole world is laid waste. Cinders flying through the air.
Caesar and Alexander and their battle-throngs.
There's hardly a trace of Tara. Troy's barely there.
The English themselves will shortly be moving along.

4

Rather than adjourn to a gin palace for which so many yearned
Joseph Mary Plunkett has adjourned
to the GPO, where the O'Rahilly's now doing his utmost
to shove himself from pillar to post
in his newfound zeal to throw off the English yoke
and settle our old score.
On Sackville Street, a girl who seemed to be about to choke
has coughed up something from her very core.
She wipes her mouth on her jute cloak
and reloads her grandfather's four-bore.
The sky is full of coal dust. The old order's overturned.
Caesar and Alexander. Their massed hosts.
Tara was burned. Troy was burned.
One of these days the English will give up the ghost.

5

I've watched Countess Markievicz striding through the oaks
where our aspirations turn out to be pigs in pokes.
This rifle was used against the Muslim sepoys in Cawnpore
before being turned on the Boers
but that its firing pin
is sticking is a sign of a more general morass
in which we founder. The thin
red line at Balaclava is testimony less to the officer class
than the rank and file. The din
of the sacking of Sackville Street. Looters. Broken glass.
The world laid waste. The wind heavy with smoke.
Alexander the Great. Great Caesar. Their assorted corps.
Tara is buried under grass. Even Troy's defenses broke.
In the case of the English, much the same lies in store.

6

MacDonagh's tapping out some rhythmic verse on a biscuit tin.
In Cawnpore, the sepoys were each sewn into a pigskin
before being hanged en masse.
On Stephen's Green we got a whiff of that chlorine gas
with its distinctive pepper-pineapple smell.
The meadow pipit was shaking from stern to stem
as she pointed to the shell

of the cuckoo's egg she'd been condemned
to billet. As a dead horse's belly swells
it pushes a sniper out of his nest. Into murder and mayhem.
The wind all smut and smoor. The world spins
out of control. Alexander and Caesar. Their gangs under grass
like Tara of the Kings. Have you seen the shape Troy's in?
As for the English, that cup, too, will pass.

7

Daniel O'Connell. O'Donovan Rossa. Charles Stewart Parnell.
Patrick Pearse is sounding his own death knell
as that gob of phlegm
shines on the pavement in Sackville Street. A little gem.
On Stephen's Green, one rare moment of mirth
comes with the daily cease-fire in which a keeper feeds the dank
ducks on their dank pond. For ourselves, there's a dearth
of humor. "Leave your jewels in the bank,"
the Countess told the girls. "The only thing worth
wearing's a revolver." It seems she shot one officer point-blank.
The whole world's foundering. A smoke trail tells
of the fates of Caesar, Alexander. Those who kissed their hems.
Tara's plowed under. Troy eventually fell.
Surely the English will get what's coming to them?

8

The dead horse's swollen belly has now so tightened its girth
it looks as if it might give birth
to a replica of itself. In an effort to outflank
us the English have banged out a tank
from the smokeboxes of two locomotives. The men with a hand
on the tiller were so familiar with Tory Sound
they thought nothing of taking command
of the Asgard. To be renowned on Tory is to be
    world-renowned.
From a burst sandbag a skein of sand
winds as it's unwound.
The air tastes of grit. The world offers no safe berth.
Tsar Alexander. The Kaiser. Their serried ranks.
Tara is debased. You see how deep Troy lies beneath the earth.
The very English will sink as all those sank.

9

Those who can't afford a uniform may wear a blue armband
from which the meadow pipit filches a single strand
to bind its nest. The rest of us are bound
by honor alone. The English pound
the GPO while we ourselves meet brute strength with brute
determination. The pipit interweaves wondrous blue
and that workaday sandbag jute.

That the O'Rahilly was the last to know of the impending to-do
but first to execute
the plan of attack is ever so slightly skewed.
The world's topsy-turvy, though. This dust's the dust that fanned
Caesar and Alexander as each gained ground.
Tara's under pasture. At Troy, it's clear how things stand.
For the English, perhaps, their time will come around.

Avalon

When it came to earning another stripe
back there on "apple island"
our lieutenants knew those splotches in the rafters
were splotches of gangrene and gore

and opportunity was "rife" rather than "ripe."
The rank and file had fallen silent
since we'd held out the idea of heaven or the hereafter.
The main thing in their future was a war

for which the press gangs of the Grenadiers
were already recruiting.
In the orchard behind the farm

it was becoming increasingly clear
one apple tree might be on something like a firm footing
while another was merely chancing its arm.

July 1, 1916: With the Ulster Division

1

You have to wonder why one old ram will step
out along a turf bank on the far side of Killeeshil, his feet raw
from a bad case of rot,
while another stays hunched under his cape
of sackcloth or untreated sheepskin.
That memory's urgent as a skelf
in my big toenail, or a nick
in my own ear, drawing me back
to a boghole where black water swirled
and our blaze-faced mare
sank to her hocks. For even as I grasped a camouflage net
hanging over the dressing station in Clairfaye Farm
I thought of the halt and lame
who, later today, must be carried along a trench
named Royal Avenue, who'll find themselves entrenched
no less physically than politically. I think now of young O'Rawe
of the Royal Irish Rifles, barely out of step
though he digs with the wrong foot. I see him on Hodge's farm
of a winter morning, the sun hinting like a tin
of bully beef from a high shelf
in the officers' quarters. A servant boy tugging at the hayrick
for an armful of fodder. At least we'll be spared the back-

breaking work of late August in a flax dam, the stink unfurled
like a banner across the moor
where greatcoated bodies ret.
I think of Giselle, her flaxen hair in a net,
who served me last week in a village café, teaching me the game
of the goose even as she plucked a gander's cape.

2

At a table in Giselle's café one orderly was painting a landscape
in yellow ocher, raw sienna, and raw
umber, pausing once in a while to gnaw at a tranche
of thick-skinned Camembert. Something about that estaminet
where I had tried a soupçon of gin
from an eggcup made of delf
made me intolerably homesick.
The music the orderly played on the Victrola was Offenbach's
Overture from *Orpheus in the Underworld*.
It was as if a servant girl from Vermeer
were pouring milk to steep
the bread for panady, Giselle lighting my cigarette
as Hodge himself once set a flame
to a paraffin lamp in the cowshed on that valuable farm
of land in Killeeshil. Later this morning I'll shoulder my firearm
and fall in as a raw
recruit with the veterans who followed the Boers from the Cape
of Good Hope to the Orange Free State like rats

following the Pied Piper of Hamelin
in search of gold and pelf.
That officer from the Rifles carried a blackthorn stick.
The wound in his back
brought to mind a poppy, of all things. Something has curled
up and died in the quagmire
of the trench
named Sandy Row down which the boys will surely step
on the Twelfth of July. It's a shame
it was only last week I met Giselle and fell into her amorous net.

3

You have to wonder at the zeal with which some drive a bayonet
through a straw-
stuffed effigy of Lundy. It'll be no distance to Clairfaye Farm
from Thiepval Wood. It'll be one step
forward into no-man's-land between the Ghibellines
and Guelphs
with their little bags of tricks, *ich, ich*—
one step forward, two steps back
towards the Schwaben Redoubt. I noticed how O'Rawe twirled
his mustache as he sang Tom Moore's
"Let Erin Remember." Commanding officers in sheepskin capes
are under orders not to leave the trench
and go over the top. It's the duty of the rest of us to seek fame
and fortune. The needle had stuck in a rut

on the Victrola halfway through a fox-trot.

The blaze-faced mare Hodge bought from a farmer in Ardstraw,

the ram from a farmer in Tydavnet.

It seems now everywhere I go there's a trench

that's precisely as tall and thin

as my own good self

and through which, if I march double quick,

I may yet find my way back

to bounteous Killeeshil, the bog from which I was hurled

into this bog. There's a strong chance that Giselle, *mon amour*,

will hold me hostage in my bed at Clairfaye Farm

and simply not allow me to escape.

For the moment I must concentrate on taking aim

as I adjust my helmet and haversack and mount the firing step.

Wilfred Owen: November 4, 1918

What I had taken for the warble of a bird
now had me brood
on those finch- and nuthatch-furtive hedgerows
of my dreamed-of childhood, kedgeree
and eggs-and-soldiers on parade
at breakfast, a parrot
quick-stepping along its perch,
a creeping barrage
of rain, *pace* Siegfried Sassoon,
whereby every season was monsoon season,
rain falling back on itself
when threatened with a countersalvo
from the chestnut trees
and, worst of all, my dearies,
casting a pall over our afternoon game of tennis,
the decapitated Saint Denis
bearing his head before him like a cooling cake,
like an apricot-breast borne by the brambling or "cock
o' the north."
Now I wondered how on earth
what I took for the warble of a bird
might, in fact, be a duckboard
twittering underfoot
as I embarked on a final feat

of balance across the gurgle
of mud, my chest stretched like a coracle
over its willow ribs . . .
In olden times an Irish king would part his robes
and proffer his right nipple
to a subservient noble . . .
I met him just once, Robert Graves,
in the sacred willow groves
of Midlothian, where he expressed something like guilt
about having to kill his fellow Celts
from east of the Rhine.
A krater is merely a cup filled with watered-down wine.
Now the Germans have mastered
the deployment of chlorine gas and mustard,
I expect the chances are slender
this is not, in fact, the whistle from a gas cylinder
that bruits and noises itself abroad
but the warble, my dearies, the warble of a bird.

Armistice Day

In a northern forest the very ravens
were flagging as you raised another glass
of the rakija you'd inherited from that dodgy Sarajevan.
Until last night the only song you'd sung
was granite, granite, granite.
Even then we were far from close
to finding common ground.
You looked beyond this unlikely haven
to wonder how the negotiators could be clean-shaven.
Perhaps a distant captain would give tongue
to a hope to which you'd clung.

This morning there's a gearing
up to settle on a single term
for "a forest clearing
that will accommodate a high-strung
railway car."
That car is lodged here as Saint Fiacre's arm
is lodged within its arm-shaped reliquary.
We look beyond the goal to which we're steering
to wonder if it isn't met by veering.
Perhaps a distant patois will give tongue
to a hope to which we've clung.

Far to the south, among the wolf-infested
dunes and salt ponds
of Landes, two sheepskin-vested
shepherds will climb down from their single-rung
five-foot pine stilts
long enough to suspend
hostilities.
They'll look beyond the scrub they've readily breasted
to wonder if they've finally been bested.
Perhaps a distant she-wolf will give tongue
to a hope to which they've clung.

Edward Elgar: Cello Concerto
in E Minor (1919)

1

Valiant old spearman, old Elgar
of the high-gloss
finish, of the lacquer
smooth as glass

albeit derived from a coarse resin
itself derived from a tree-bug.
You'd long been able to refine
your experience against the Ninth Legion

into the ability to roughen
your style in that same region.
It stands to reason
a spear that's been at your beck

and call for ten centuries
of shield-walls
thrown up against all and sundry
might now resonate with the wails

of this one squaddy
picked at random from the orchestra,
with a rail-thin human body
in its death throes.

2

Valiant old spearman, old Elgar
of the mead-hall,
swapping that honey liquor
for a mud-hole

filled with urine
on the outskirts of Passchendaele.
You'd fritter and frolic
among daffodils and dandelions

and take time by the forelock
with the hunter, Orion.
It transpires his bow is backed with iron.
The bow-edge is dull

from the downward spiral
of forces once spryly mustered
that are now all splatter and sprawl.
The freshly delivered mustard

gas is already
taking its toll on these tearful
boy-soldiers trying to hold steady
for the next interval.

3

Valiant old spearman, old Elgar,
stalwart and staunch
against such forces as beleaguer
us here in the stench

of the dunghill
on which we've been thrown.
You'd been all but delirious
when you heard from across the Channel

the British and German artilleries
vie for a place in the annals.
It was somewhere there in the tangle
of duckboards and open drains

so many had struck a bargain
with history,
having once and for all broken
rank in a tumble of pale straw

and cadmium yellow.
Somewhere near Ypres
your own blood-burnished cello
must have fallen facedown in barbed wire.

At Tuam

Among the hundreds of children who stare up at us from their
    septic tank
is James Muldoon, who died in 1927
at the age of four months. At least he would never be forced
    to thank

the Lord for mercies large or small. That cry to high heaven
must come from Brendan Muldoon, who died in 1943
at a mere five weeks. A teenage nun bows before an unleavened

host held up by a priest like a moon held up by an ash tree.
In 1947 the eleven-month-old Bridget Muldoon, a namesake
    of the mother
who would shortly give birth to me,

has already distinguished herself as being a bit of a bother
while Dermott Muldoon, three months old in 1950, is about
    to join the ranks
of my foster-sisters and foster-brothers

in that unthinkable world where a wasp may recognize another
    wasp's face
and an elephant grieve for an elephant down at the watering
    place.

Likely to Go Unnoticed

Amid acres of rapeseed, a streak of ragwort
may yet shine
as an off-the-record
remark becomes the party line,

as a dray in saddle-pad and blinders
doing shit work
on the streets outsplendors
the Byerley Turk,

as a yellow truck that's missed its exit
on a roundabout (a dearth
of signage?) repeats one word—

HORSES—at which it has itself but guessed.
The roundabout's named after Maria Edgeworth
of Edgeworthstown, County Longford.

Robert Lowell at Castletown House

1

This afternoon the chimney made a clean breast
of the matter as Caroline and he took turns
to argue for her hightailing it to London. Tomorrow he'll fly
    west
to Lizzie, her own recalcitrance

the recalcitrance of a mare that will kick out
because she's too often been confined to the stable
"for her own good."
As it is, he's managed at once to disable

the burglar alarm and lock
himself in. He picks up the phone to hear his father mutter
something about Lafcadio Hearn

in a closet. The night is coming at a lick
across the stubble-fields even as the downpipe from a gutter
is mouthing the word "rain."

2

Everything that went against the grain.
Everything that had rattled its chain.
Everything that had gone down the drain
because of the lack of a little salt in the brain.

3

The spot where the Vartry River meets the sea should be a
    marsh
yet the going yesterday had been firm
enough till he somehow crossed Caroline, his penalty so harsh
it was handed down in cuneiform

by Ur-Nammu. He hangs on the cusp
between a wood nymph from the Age of Fable
and a self-styled "gossip"
from Kentucky. The transatlantic telegraph cable

turns out to have been spun from straw.
Even it's slightly unhinged, the shutter.
When one's weighing wives one must sometimes set a thumb

on the scale. Though it had been all washed up in the estuary,
leaving high and dry both cabin cruiser and cutter,
the ocean was back to throwing dirt on him.

4

Partly because the chances were slim
her light would ever but briefly dim
it had seemed, after vodkas and Pimm's,
the moon might still love nothing more than a midnight swim.

5

The amount of molasses one might add to her warm bran mash
would generally take its tone
from how a mare has handled the hundred-yard dash
towards the ha-ha. What if the Palladian

golden ratio might apply to gin and vermouth? The empty grate
is a castoff and the card table
itself a discard.
Now there's a smoke stain on the gable

and it looks as if night has already fallen at the first fence.
In the long gallery a candle sputters
like yet another sylph.

That glass chandelier, meanwhile, was shipped from Venice
in a cask of butter
so as to save it from itself.

April in New Hope

Ascribe it though we may to the McCormick clan
the technology of the mechanical reaper and hay tedder
had been developed by the Celts
before being lost with Rome. A Cambridge man
might be done for by a "bedder"
but Princeton men kept slaves. In 1849, the Corn Belt

still stretched to the Delaware.
We few, we happy few, are still so newfangled
with our own Henriad
we forget New Hope is where
each generation is doomed to wrangle
the shad roe from the shad

only to pair them once again, fried in bacon fat
and served on a white platter
with capers and lime.
By 1949, Richard Feynman was already plugging away at
the idea of antimatter being matter
that merely goes backwards in time.

A Chickadee in Riverside Park

1

I was insisting "athwart" has been a synonym for "crosswise"
at least since Helgi Hrólfsson laid claim to his sand spit.
We were just drawing level with the Port Authority
as per our usual routine
when the storm broke.
A money manager manages a heist
by standing on the shoulders of a client
the way snow relies on an evergreen
to make itself look good.
The "cowling" is a kind of engine-hood,
just as the engine-hood is itself a take
on Helgi's lapstrake.
My sense is that the fuselage of the old De Havilland
was stitched together from birch bark.
The term "deiced"
dates only from the early 1930s.
In 1940, when W. C. Fields and Mae West rode into Little
   Bend,
passengers were still on a Grand Tour
and flight attendants wore haute couture
and smoked a Turkish blend.
"I think I could eat one of Bellamy's veal pies"

is a line no older than the Younger Pitt
but a chickadee in Riverside Park
has been hanging in there since the time of Christ.

2

You saw how a hammer striking a wrist-spike may spark
a clash of reason and emotion worthy of Kleist.
You saw how a high-rise casting a shadow
at 3:15
over the newly mopped floor
of the midtown map
encouraged us to be more energy compliant.
A chickadee doesn't so much preen
as congratulate itself on having withstood
the charms of an armoire finished in plywood
that no less wants to shake
off being likened to Icelandic layer cake
than being popularly known as "blond"
abandoned on the sidewalk by a three-legged chair.
A stopgap
forsythia exclaims *Cuidado!*
as if, heaven forefend,
we were about to happen on mastodon spoor
and a steaming pile of mastodon manure
at 107th and West End.
It looks as if Matthew, Luke, and John all followed Mark

in conflating the centurions who diced
for Jesus's camel-hair
jacket with those off-duty policemen shooting craps.

3

You have to admit it's with a certain flair
the chickadee tips its skullcap
at the idea of Golgotha bleeding into Gotham.
As is clear from the fossil record of the Pliocene,
North America has twice
been settled by the tit
so the chickadee is superdefiant,
venting its spleen
to the assembled mob. I knew you'd
remember the true cross only is known as the Rood.
The crowd that wants to break
W. C. Fields on a wheel may settle for burning him at the stake.
Not only a little chickadee may vent
at the threat from these darkening skies
of another hit.
Blossom-snow from a sky-gash? Perhaps snow-blossom
bucking the trend?
The one thing I know for sure
is how rarely our motives are pure.
Even Jesus wondered if he was a godsend

or had merely become ensnared
in a pyramid scheme. Merely become entrapped.
You saw how the tower crane used to build the high-rise
is now enshrined in it.

The Door

Though it beggars belief
there's something more

than this realm
of smoke

and mirrors, it does seem
an inescapable

fact that a nub
of ash in a cartwheel-hub,

a hornbeam
paddle, a maple

butcher's block, an elm
cutting board, and an oak

table-leaf
have all shown me the door.

With Eilmer of Malmesbury

In memory of Jack Eustis (1998–2014)

In Paddington a man allows his upright bass
to rest its head on his shoulder—
the awkward embrace
of a father and teenage son. I think of one who smolders

in a flame as I take the train
to Swindon, from there a cab to the Old Bell Hotel,
the oldest in England. Since the unusually large brain
of an Apache war chief will swell

even more when boiled, an army surgeon saws
through Mangas's brain stem, tipping it into a vermeil
basin for further study. It was from watching jackdaws
avail of the thermals

over this scarp that Eilmer got it into his head he might
take off from the church tower.
This was in 1000 AD, or thereabouts, so his flight
was a testimony to Eilmer's staying power

even though he went no more than two hundred yards.
He fell, broke both legs, and was "lame ever after."
My friends' beloved son also fell hard
from a rafter

but stopped short
of the floor. An eleventh-century Benedictine monk
was given a daily allowance of a quart
of soup in which to dunk

bread made from barley and spelt.
We don't know if Eilmer flew with the aid of feathers
or a contraption of linen and silk. The belt
worn by a Benedictine was made of leather

but a Franciscan's cincture was rope. The gaudy sleeve
I once put on is fraying by the hour.
At a distance of three thousand miles I grieve
with my friends. An E minor on a bass sours

even as it soars through the skull of Mangas Coloradas.
When I look down I see the pall cast over everything
is only partly the shadow
of my own wing.

Plume

On the outskirts of Reykjavik I find myself slapping the ass
of a thick-piled Viking horse,
sending up a plume of dust and gas

that all but obscures the scrawl
on parchment of a jet plane, sending up a pall
the likes of which I don't recall

since a ruse
I pulled on my mother. This one involved my father
lying in hospital, much the worse

for rheumatic fever,
and her abandoning my eight-year-old self at home
when she breezed off to visit him. Knowing how she favored

that canister of Yardley's talcum,
I shook it out little by little into a rug
on the floor of her bedroom

till it had vanished into thin air. Even then I was struck
by my vengefulness, by the sheer vindictiveness
of this conjuring trick,

a vindictiveness now matched by hers. She'd followed her nose
to the scene of my crime. English Lavender.
Her running noose

around my neck. Is that a touch of founder
in her nearside rear hoof? Sending up a cloud of volcanic slag
that's at once growing fainter

and more sleek.
Since it's for the most part
composed of vitreous ash, silica,

ferrous oak gall,
resentment, griefs, squabbles, and squalls
it may yet enthrall

the plane's state-of-the-art
combustion chamber, clogging the engine with molten glass
the way a poem may yet stop the heart.

Hunting with Eagles, Western Mongolia, 2016

1

Only when an eagle has recovered from her summer molt
and the larch lost its needles
may the hunt begin in earnest. Our breakfast of mutton in mild
broth with broad rice noodles

should tide us over till lunch;
that the eagle herself is working on an empty belly
explains her chirruping and why, given the chance to launch
herself off a ridge, she'll usually fall for the ploy

of a strip of sheep-lung lodged in Agalai's glove
and promptly fly to him. Eagle on arm, Agalai steers his pony
straight up the face of a cliff
while we continue to skirt the base. My 100 percent yak-wool
    beanie

and 100 percent yak-wool sweater might stand me in better
    stead
against the wind were there not still snow
on the far peaks. Myself and four other beaters study
the valley floor for a news-

flash from one of the red foxes
that prey on sheep and goats. And that goes directly to the point
of training an eagle in the first place, why Agalai fixes
on her head a little leather bonnet

like a scold's cap, removing it only so her sharp
eye may glimpse,
beyond the sagebrush and other shrubs,
a totality of sorts. As Agalai releases her she climbs

an air current the better to scry
the fox we flush from cover only to watch it scurry
across the scree like a wraith
of itself before almost straightaway going to earth.

2

Maybe it's somewhere near this spot that the drama
of the burial of Genghis Khan
unfolded. The talk last night was all of Clinton and Trump,
the US refusal to allow Bin Laden to become an icon

by burying him in a secret grave, then cutting out the tongues
of the burial party. At the dead center
of my ger is a stove that burns 100 percent yak dung
and dry sticks. Last night I was worried a cinder

might set fire to a wall-
hanging woven from some of the finest wool
from some of the finest lambs that ever gamboled
in this vale—hangings the more compelling for being incomplete.

3

That these ornate wall-hangings fall short of the raked soil
of the ger floor is meant to symbolize our fallings short
right along the sill
of the world. My guide was shrewd

enough to know my horse might have a mind
to be persnickety and had lengthened my stirrups
accordingly to make it easier to dismount.
Even at this remove we could hear the eagle's chirrups

cut short as she was once again bent
upon a fox. Once again we watched it lope
out of view. Once again the bond
endured and the eagle flew to Agalai, paying more than lip

service to the idea that we live from precipice to precipice,
that a hope quickly kindled
may be as quickly quenched. Now we've stopped for lunch I
     pose
with the eagle on a gauntlet

and persuade myself I belong
to the line of *berkutchi* in a Bronze Age petroglyph
who first held out the hope of a strip of sheep-lung.
Surely a forebear of this eagle would have served the Caliph

of Baghdad? Because of the prowess
as hunters of her lineage,
this is but one of successive chicks Agalai has gone back to
    prise
from the same ledge-nest. Only when she seems to lunge

at me with a halfhearted yelp
do I sense just how precipitously she might elbow
me out. A primrose cere highlighting her pewter beak,
she grips my arm as if about to let me in on something really
    big.

A Tortoise

Try telling a dramatist the sky's the limit
when an eagle has let fall a tortoise onto his bare skull.
Now Aeschylus will expire
without the opportunity to develop his skill
in single combat

or master basic hero-feats.
However emotionally detached,
a tortoise had it within it to be the sound box of a lyre
improvised by my friend, Joseph, in a last-ditch
effort to rise above the Gulag.

Given the Portuguese regained the fortress at Almeida
after the Treaty of Paris
it's clear not every outcome is dire.
That's why, though the tortoise pretends to browse
the chessboard, its every move's a gambit.

A tortoise will put its best foot
forward on the baize
and strike out across a scum-covered quagmire
with all the poise
of a high-functioning alcoholic.

Yet this same tortoise has covered its ass with its helmet
like a grunt
in a helicopter-gunship coming under fire
from that contested ground
near the border of Vietnam and Cambodia.

Aubade

At 1:00 a.m. the dairy sink
in your yard was a deer-glyphed megalith
caught in my headlights.
I found not only sermons
in stones but Tamurlane of Samarkand
in the Timberland mukluks
tossed on your bedroom floor.
Now I'd rather shop for staples
(bread, milk, Clorox),
at the twenty-four-hour Supermart
than lag
behind the laggard
dawn about to steal
from haystack to haystack, no less bent

on taking us to the brink
of destruction than was Clement V
on the Knights
Templar. He was determined
to disband
that herd of ten-point bucks
by showing them the door
courtesy of a papal
bull he dubbed "*Vox*

in excelso." For I'm averse, sweetheart,
to ever again seeing a stag
take the head staggers,
ever again seeing dawn kneel
as if it might repent,

as if it might come to think
of itself as a figure from some ancient myth—
Mesopotamian? Hittite?
Greek? German?—
throwing up its hands
with the dumbstruck
oaks or shaking to their cores
the Japanese maples,
unyoking the great ox
from the straw-laden cart
even as it divines the hag
in the haggard,
then putting its shoulder to the wheel
it means to reinvent.

Wave

In memory of C. K. Williams

I happened to be putzing around in the Gellert Spa in Budapest
while you did your very best

to hold on to the world-brim.
Saint Gellert taking a last look over the rim

of his nail-studded barrel. I was stretched in a thermal bath
even as Syrian refugees struggled to find a path

across the border at Zakay. Two of the many top-of-the-line
treatments on offer featured red wine

and chocolate. It was in Peru, Vermont,
in the late eighties I first heard you vaunt

Vallejo and Neruda. You were so tall I could no more reach you
for a farewell hug than scale the Heights of Machu Picchu.

My own ancestors had floated down the Danube
on a combination of a pigskin inner tube

and a somewhat overblown
sense not only of their own

expertise in cooperage and smelting copper
and telling whopper after whopper

but the intrinsic importance of things
Celtic. In the National Museum of Hungary I gaped at rings

with intricate spirals much as I'd once admired
the wedding band Catherine made for you. I lay now in my hired

canary swimming togs in an outdoor pool, a pool renowned
for being the first to feature a wave machine. The burial mound

of the Dohány Street synagogue dates from 1945.
From time to time a big-breasted woman has been known to dive

into the headwaters of the Danube and return to the fold
in Ireland itself, between the Paps of Danu. The mire and mold

of the world would become your subjects, of course,
be it the Hun buried astride his horse

with a rusted bell and garnet-encrusted gold
paraphernalia or the Dohány Street mound that holds

the bodies of two thousand Jews starved by the Arrow Cross.
Except for fifteen minutes in the hour the wave machine is at a
    loss

as to how it's persevered
since 1927. Almost ninety years, Charlie. Almost ninety years.

That it will be starting soon
is announced, it would seem, by a little signature tune

on the speakers. In addition to those forced to march
from here to Austria, so many more would pass under the arch

in Auschwitz-Birkenau. The peril
that faced Saint Gellert when his nail-spiked barrel

went trundling down the hill
would be amplified until

the needle bent. When I'd blithely asked Catherine to replicate
your silver ring it hadn't struck me you and I would mate

for life like Herr Tukhus and Frau Tukhus.
Were it not for the lining of mucus

a poet's mind, like a stomach, will happily digest itself.
I'd left my silver wedding band on the shelf

in cabin 108 to protect it from sulfur, oblivious to the fact
that even such temerity, such tact

as you'd always shown—
the grace that had, if anything, grown—

wouldn't help you at the world-brim,
wouldn't stave off that grimmest of grim

rollouts, wouldn't save
you from the force of that much anticipated, unexpected wave.

Superior Aloeswood

In memory of Leonard Cohen

I light a stick of Superior Aloeswood
from the box you gave me on South Tremaine
when last I visited. You'd conducted us through your new CD,
Professor Bob and myself tapping out a rhythm
on our cans of soda
while Nicodemus and Joseph of Arimathea
stayed back in the mix. Even as the aloeswood's musk-sweet
drifts through my kitchen I determine

how determinedly you refused to blend
a sorrow-base with a top note of solace.
Hard to make light of Bashar al-Assad turning his bombardiers
on his own citizenry (*grâce à* Putin),
while our vain, vindictive Pompadour
is pushing every button
on the console. During their break at the processing plant
the Mexicans are celebrating All Souls'

with chilaquiles, there being no circumstance so bland
a little extra salsa
won't kick it up. That August afternoon in Tinseltown
we touched on how Europe's

right-wing nationalism is so in tune
with our own. The one note produced by the jaw harps
was more than enough for the Jews of Poland,
most of them conveyed from Silesia

to Auschwitz-Birkenau only after ponying up
for their own tickets.
Though we'd hoped to meet at the Blue Plate Oysterette
you'd been confined to barracks
on account of the side effects, I surmised, of steroids.
Not periwinkles, Nicodemus. Periwigs!
And though they went for five dollars a pop
I used to favor a half dozen Belons from the Damariscotta

over a dozen Wellfleets. Hard not to think of Pip,
the cabin boy of the *Pequod*,
forced to eat all that traif.
Hard not to think of him learning to flense
blubber from a whale like a turf-cutter cutting turf
on his smallholding. There was a little flourish on the violins
when you so graciously offered myself and Professor Bob
some Cheddar or aged Gouda

and I happened to ask if you were a fan of Époisses—
the "King of Cheeses,"
according to Brillat-Savarin. I must have been in manic
mode when I'd have Murray's FedEx you a round

only hours after getting back to New York. A Cistercian monk
has been known to obsessively rinse the rind
in the pomace brandy that gives it such extra pizzazz.
Why the electorate chooses

the likes of Ronald Bonzo and George W. Bozo
as Commander-in-Chief has already defied exegesis.
Hard not to think of Starbuck opening the waterproof match keg
and contriving to light a lamp of hope
while Tashtego, Daggoo, and Queequeg
despair of the vengeful Ahab.
When Nicodemus busies
himself treating the body of Jesus

"with a mixture of myrrh and aloes,
about a hundred pound weight,"
this "aloes" is our self-same aloeswood, beaten to a pulp
and thereafter prized
as an embalming agent from Beirut through Bologna to Bilbao.
It seems particularly appropriate that a priest
should also distill brandy from the lees
of wine. Not one iota

of aloeswood shall derive from the *Aquilaria* tree
till it's threatened by a mold.
Only when a gold-orange
bloom of bacteria is allowed to seep

through a rind-washed cheese is its raunchy
essence revealed. Only when a sponge on a stalk of hyssop
is proffered him does Christ acknowledge the glitter
of the doubloon nailed to the mast is both amulet

against the whale and emblem of Burgundian caseiculture.
"Trouble is," you e-mailed
in October of your new favorite, Époisses,
"it's the only thing I want to eat."
Only when it's threatened does the *Aquilaria* push
back with the fragrant gum that translates to agar or oud.
Egoless, aquiline, *égalitaire*,
you yourself had tried no less to emulate

the teachings of the abbot of Mount Baldy
than his famous locum,
Bernard of Clairvaux. I suspect Bernard had a hand
in the development of the Meursault
Jefferson would come to love. Hard to reconcile the whale hunt
with the thirteen attributes of Divine Mercy
now that Ahab pilots the pilot
away from our ninth and final gam

and, having tempered his barb in the blood
of Queequeg, Tashtego, and Daggoo, offers his final l'chaim
while urging us to stand firm. A chasuble
is a version of a "little house." A kind of poncho.

It was no time after Jezebel
had married Ahab that she took it upon herself to banish
the prophets of Israel and trade them for the polity
of Baal. In the matter of leukemia,

of course, it comes down to the bone marrow
producing freak blood cells. Let's not forget how the brazen
serpent becomes a false idol
to which the Israelites cry "Hallelujah"
and make their own offerings of incense. One jot or one tittle
shall in no way pass from the law
till Abraham sacrifices Ishmael on Mount Moriah.
The incense-smoke sends up its orison

over Mounts Moriah and Meru.
That August afternoon our *tour d'horizon*
included not only the Tower of Wrong
being built by Trump
from the promises on which he'll shortly renege
but the life-size diorama
of a grove of trees. Those same trees producing myrrh
only when they're wounded. Just as the resin

in a stick of Superior Aloeswood
is produced only as an immune response
to an all-out attack. It's not only Bashar al-Assad
dropping barrel-bombs on his people that threatens the core

of our humanity. In the meantime, the sweat
from a round of Époisses raises its own Kyrie
through the kitchen to mingle with the funky incense-soot.
Not harps, Nicodemus. Not harps. Harpoons!

At the River

for Bruce Springsteen at seventy

Now the eighteen-wheeler of state has flipped
and blocked what we took for an exit ramp
and our legislative gears have been stripped
and the '69 Chevy's red taillamp
glows in Kentucky, in Wyoming glows,
our mines having seen a buildup of fire-damp
that threatens one of these fine days to blow,
and politicians, of course, still decamp
for any side on which their bread is buttered
while our food workers make do with food stamps
and our President stars in his own gutter,
the time has surely come to turn up the amp,
the Great Blue Heron taking a firm stand
on the mudflats as in the meadowlands.

It Wasn't Meant to Be Like This

It wasn't meant to be like this.
If we were destined to push the envelope
surely it was by flying a recovered Avro Arrow
above the speed of sound?
The most we were meant to condemn
was the brief resurgence of Day-Glo
in a thistle flower, given how we routinely forsook
such dazzle for the drear.
That was before spring itself was a no-show.
The fact of global warming, we must now concede,
has left us barely a coast to hug.
When we stared into the abyss

we were meant to be in something akin to a state of bliss.
We were meant to tope
the fermented fruit of a saguaro
with which a shaman absentmindedly downed
a handful of diltiazem.
We weren't supposed to uphold the status quo.
Nor were we meant to brook
such an assault on all we once held dear
by Bully Boy and Il Generalissimo.
An ounce of weed
was to represent only the idea of a gateway drug.
It wasn't meant to be like this

rerun of the ban on the Mississippi
of Huck Finn and the defense of Scopes
by Clarence Darrow.
Now the Supreme Court has likely found
against its own judgment in rem.
We expected an end to gerrymandering, Jim Crow,
winning by hook or by crook.
We were meant to somehow be in the clear.
Who knew the Russians would be once again gung ho?
Who knew Bully Boy would sell our title deed
to the thugs?
When we stared into the abyss

we were still meant to be able to reminisce
at length on the hay rope
and the horse-drawn harrow,
the hare run ragged by a rag-tongued hound,
the stately diadem
and the golden long ago.
The poem that dogged us from an old schoolbook
was to be found by a dog-ear.
Page turning was a habit we'd eventually outgrow.
Even though a newscaster sometimes buries the lead
in a whiskey fug,
it wasn't meant to be like this

spinning of platelet-tops, this trompothrombopoesis.
A radioactive isotope

should have shone through mostly in our bone marrow
rather than as the glory that crowned
an ICBM
as it shuttled to and fro.
The news is now not only gobbledygook
but geared, it seems, to what each wants to hear.
Each sits in isolation on his ice floe
with his personalized feed
of hogwash and humbug.
When we stared into the abyss

things were supposed to be slightly hit-or-miss
yet allowing us to maintain the hope
we'd not quite strayed from the straight and narrow.
We were meant to stride along the higher ground
rather than slouch towards Bethlehem.
We were inclined to fall in with things being so-so.
The thistle's beard was meant to make it look
wise beyond its years.
Not wise, exactly. Somewhat in the know.
We didn't expect "thistle seed" to be thistle seed
but we did expect to feel self-satisfied, maybe even smug.
It wasn't meant to be at all like this
when we stared into the abyss.

Position Paper

1

One rotten apple keeps the doctor away.
When the doctor's away the cat will get the cream.
The law is an ass that loves to hear itself bray.
The path of least resistance leads to Rome.

Like father, like two peas in a pod.
It's in the country of the blind
we find ourselves kissing the auld sod.
A society is great when men plant

trees in which they'll never seek shade.
Man does not live by half a loaf
while riding roughshod
over a house divided against itself.

A wolf in sheep's clothing separates the goats.
A little stroke is a dangerous thing.
There's more than one way of skinning the cat
that may look at a king.

All things come to those who get their paws wet.
A miss is as good as an Englishman's smile.
He that will have a cake out of wheat
must grind exceeding small.

2

In for a penny, in for a pound of cure.
A journey of a thousand miles begins when you hitch
your wagon to a steer. Take care
not to count your blessings before they hatch.

You can't get a quart
of what's sauce for the upped swan
into an apple cart.
Ne'er cast a clout before swine.

One swallow doesn't wallow in mud
till a pig in a poke takes flight.
Better we catch larks than one man's meat.
It's an ill wind that blows nobody a hundredfold.

3

It never rains till oil has been poured
over the troubled mill wheel's cogs.
Those who live by the sword
will die by the pen. Too many cooks

make a dish best served cold.
Cut your coat according to the moth.
In Rome, every cloud
is born with a silver spoon in its mouth

and, on its tongue, an ox.
Step on a crack, my dearies, step on a crack
and teach your granny to suck eggs
from her one basket. Beware of Greeks

bearing a gift horse
on which beggars might ride.
Little acorns do indeed have the biggest ears.
If wishes were fishes we'd all rot

from the head down forenenst a stable door.
Waste not, nothing gained.
The poor workman blames a h'a'porth of tar.
There's many a slip to every coin.

4

The plot is thicker than water off a duck's back.
From your lips is enough.
All nose-to-the-grindstone makes Jack
a dishwater-dull knife.

Where there's muck we become as sounding brass.
Put your money in the company you keep.
It takes all sorts to make a silk purse
but birds of a feather flock in your cap.

Don't even think of crossing the bridge
till it takes you to the fair.
Practice what a goat might preach.
Strike while you've got too many irons in the fire.

5

What you sow is a chip off the old block.
You can't teach an old dog and not get up with fleas.
He who pays the piper calls the kettle black.
Stolen fruit never falls far from the tree

on which no money grows.
It's not only that squeaky wheel but the sunflower seed
that gets the grease.
The proof of the pudding is out of sight

but even Homer will nod
to a blind horse or a one-eyed man.
Don't take a frying pan to crack a nut.
Burning the candle at both ends justifies the means.

When in Rome, spare the rod
and spoil the whole barrel. It's all grist
to those mills of God.
Don't count your chickens till they come home to roost.

Loose lips tie knots.
Don't put the cart before the storm.
Don't wash your dirty linen in a watched pot.
The leopard can't change horses in midstream.

A Rooster in Tepoztlán

1

Confirmed in their belief there's still a need
for worship prior to Lauds,
the street-dog choristers

insist on how
any three of them form a quorum.
However great the din

they're eventually forced to cede
their urine-soaked sod
to a single rooster,

his beak the prow
of an imperial quinquereme
at the break of dawn.

2

Not that a rooster ever rues
the day of days
he first lowered the tone

by kicking up a fuss.
He specializes in splutter and spout.
Sometimes the bearer

becomes the bad news,
as when Augustus would parlay
the cult of Diana

at Ephesus
into the out-and-out
worship of himself as emperor.

3

A rooster will pay cash on the barrel
to join the Praetorian Guard
but the flanking eagles betoken

our throwing off one yoke
even as we take on fresh burdens.
Left to his own devices, a rooster will don

the kind of gaudy apparel
more often associated with the bard—
the three-quarter-length *tuigen*

or "feather-cloak."
That he has a sense of his own importance
is hardly something he'll deny.

4

That wattle-ear was sliced
off a slave
by the self-same Simon Peter

who'd cover it with a tissue
of lies . . . The blue gel,
the iodine,

the ice-pack ice.
The pigs who've had a close shave
in the abattoir

are in such a daze
they can't tell
Gethsemane from the Garden of Eden.

5

The rooster's claws are tempered by calcium
derived from the forearm
of a devotee of Saint Francis Xavier

going for broke
as he sawed the heart from a yucca
or agave. The rooster himself would never deign

to take a shortcut to Elysium
via fermented sap. Beating his breast on a farm
is learned behavior

but the tendency to stroke
his own ego
is pretty much baked into his DNA.

6

From the top
of the rubbish tip on which he's parked
he rubbishes any duenna

trying to pull rank.
His hens are rumpled. Raggedy-ass.
Most statements issued from his pilaster

of slow-cured adobe
are followed by an exclamation mark!
A sheet of corrugated tin

is his main plank.
"When oh when," he blubbers, "will this cup pass?"
All bully-pulpitry. All bluster.

7

For it's very rarely a cup of joy,
the cup
that runneth over.

More a seed-bleed
from the agave's once-in-a-lifetime pod.
More a fairground tune

from a windup toy
winding us up
for what seems forever.

Till the street-dogs have once again treed
a god
somewhere on the outskirts of town.

Sodus

In memory of John Ashbery

A corruption of *assorodus*, a Cayuga term meaning "silver
    wave,"
your birthplace confirmed your calling as a Lake Poet,
caged as you were in that house on Lake Road
till poetry extended you a wing.
A white wing, surely, in anticipation of the whitecap of your
    hair,
spume setting off the unfathomable blue of your eyes.
The word "whitecap" was first used by Ben Franklin
in a celebrated letter on oil and troubled water.
That was in 1773, when the term *assorodus* still had some
    currency.

With Joseph Brant in Canajoharie

In memory of Richard Wilbur

I stood with Brant in Canajoharie
where the Mohawk River finds its way through that narrow pass
and into "the pot that washes itself."
We'd already scrubbed our tin plates with sand
and were now enjoying an infusion based on chokecherries,
red willow, and sweetgrass.
"The river," he gestured, "has it within it to slough off

the detritus of the age—boatloads of beaver pelts, bales
of barley straw and salt hay amassed
by Palatine hay-hoarders,
truck beds, sandalwood, pig lead, corn bottled and canned,
home truths, veritable stockpiles
of oil and natural gas
to which we once imagined ourselves inheritors,

French hens, turtledoves, submarine-launched Tomahawks,
relics of auld decency such as the demitasse
from which I drank coffee when I found myself in the halfpenny
place with George III, grandees who grandstand,
diktat-spouting demagogues,
Big Mouth Billy Bass
mouthing 'Take Me to the River,' cargoes of ebony

and dry persimmons, Eliza Pinckney's indigo dress, Indiankillers
who believe in the idea of an underclass
that threatens our egalitarian
principles, white supremacists sporting swastika armbands,
dead batteries, old tires, fridges, Styrofoam beer coolers,
kudos-seekers, kiss-ass
Republican senators—all swilling about in that cauldron

just as back when I was in my prime
and dined here almost exclusively on bear fat flavored with
    sassafras.
The river still comes in at a rampage, still goes out as a runnel.
It persuades me that our native land
may seem to be filled to the brim—
may seem, indeed, to have reached an almost total impasse—
yet retains the capacity for its own renewal."

Putsch

Though we've scoured the realm
of oak and elm
for their bright dyestuffs,

on the first of May
it's a leg of gray
our queen has birled.

Battleship gray, to be precise.
In mothballs, on ice,
we huff and puff

as we dance on the spot
while more potshots
are fired, more insults hurled.

For in Belfast we found the will
to remain at a standstill
when General Gruff

instituted his shoot-to-kill
policy in the Antrim hills.
The wind-drums whirled. The wind-pipes skirled.

In Sharon Springs,
meanwhile, I sight a king
only in the bronze cloak and neck ruff

of a wild turkey and his mate
as they rotate
the planet with their unfurled

claws . . . Having lost her crown
to the browns,
the black and tans, the buffs,

a hummingbird
has this morning set her little outboard
motor to the world.

Frolic and Detour

The house wren, like the house sparrow
and the common spink,
is known to punch above his weight. Troglodyte, tinsmith in his
    burrow,
his *tink tink, tink tink*

bespeaking a familiarity with the science of iron-carbon alloys
the Chinese developed alongside the Dao,
he's believed to anticipate the lice
that will infest his nest by stitching into

its brush-pile the egg sacs of lice-eating spiders. The going had
    been firm,
it's also believed, till government agents broke the seal
on the clouds over Max Yasgur's dairy farm.
Robert Lowell, writing of Thomas Merton's career in
    Commonweal,

praised it as "varied and spectacular," his own tendency to
    power-grab
implicit in that phrase. Toil nor spin, Bobbie. Spin nor toil.
Lowell knew that to be the center of attention is to be the crab
at a New England crab boil,

yet he would be sad, surely, to find himself bringing up the
    rear
to Robert P. Lowell of Virginia Tech, a research pioneer in the
    huge sulfide-
mounds thrown up around ocean-floor vents. Though it's rare
for me to deviate

from the task in hand, as I drove by Saugerties I noticed how
    Bill Graham
is even now obscured by a Marshall stack, despite his having
    lined
up the dairy farm's crème de la crème—
the Who, Jimi Hendrix, Joe Cocker. I marked, too, how the
    lark and linnet

sing their psalms
in *dán díreach* whilst mine represent a departure
of sorts. One exhibition I really must catch in the Iroquois
    Indian Museum
at Howes Cave is "Walking the Steel: From Girder

to Ground Zero." *O-du-na-mis-sug-ud-da-we-shi* ("makes a
    big noise
for its size") is the Ojibwa term for the house wren, which
    builds in a bucket,
an abandoned beehive, a hangman's noose,
leaving on the lintel of each that time-release packet

of a spider-cocoon. When Tamanend, the Delaware sagamore,
shows up like a glitch
in the plot of *The Last of the Mohicans*, he leads us through
the mire
and points us to a clutch

of five porcelain eggs with ferrous
speckles and splotches. Vis-à-vis scrap-metal haulers like
Saccomanno
and Vanzetti, I'm quite disinclined to theorize
on how they lost their business acumen,

preferring to withdraw to the spa town of Sharon Springs
and fill a dumpster hired from Fred's with cast-off drapes and
drainpipes.
After the success of "Wild Thing,"
the Troggs are set on another "fucking number one." Spin nor
toil, Bobbie.

Toil nor spin. In 1677 Kaelcop, clan-leader of the
Amorgarickakan,
had sold the site of Saugerties for a piece of cloth, an English
sgraffito jar,
a loaf of bread, a shirt. In 2017 we might throw in a bargain
set of three Adirondack chairs,

a tin pail, a Black & Decker belt-sander,
and the first paperback edition of Nancy Isenberg's *White
    Trash.*
A bird spotted recently in the environs of the Walmart
    distribution center
is the elusive Bicknell's thrush

while American robins hang out at 204 Main,
the restaurant where Norm Phenix goes out of his way to wrap
Medjool dates in temptingly thick-cut bacon. On the Spanish
    Main,
meanwhile, Captain Hook lets rip

from Disney's *Peter Pan* of 1953. I'd just as soon not be
    sidetracked
by further allusions to popular culture,
but the missing component, the "fucking fairy dust" the Troggs
will "throw over the bastard," is surely of a piece with Tinker
    Bell's glitter.

2

Siding as I must with the Iroquois in their struggle against the
    Huron
I've enlisted the spirit of Tamanend
to track down the identity of an actress, "Jenny Wren,"
who's credited with playing Tinker Bell in the first West End

production of *Peter Pan*. *Homo troglodytes* was a term
   devised by Linnaeus
for a division of apedom with which he saw us being in
   dialogue,
something along the lines
of the cave dwellers who first distinguished the metallic

taste of chalybeate from sulfur and magnesium. I'll hit the
   Beekman Boys
for goats' cheese, the mall for ibuprofen,
The New York Times, bird feed, Bacardi, and bok choy.
Huron is itself a derogatory term, meaning either "ruffian"

or "boar's head," on account of the rake
of their bear-greased bristles and their supposed disdain
for the elegance once favored here on the banks of Brimstone
   Creek.
For there was a time when Sharon Springs was no less tony

than Saratoga or Tunbridge Wells,
even if ladies of quality were still on the hunt
for new ways with bones and feathers. It turns out the "Wal"
in Walmart goes back to Sam Walton. Though I've no wish to
   lose a hand

to a gas chain saw, à la J. M. Barrie,
there's a Hifashion model on clearance at four hundred dollars
   off the list

price that has me sorely tempted. The problem with "heavy-
     duty" power-
sander belts is that they last

no longer than a leaf
in a Black & Decker leaf blower. What has the house wren
     seeing red
is that the silk lining of a 1920s bridal glove
he found in the dumpster may not be so readily wrought

into a nest until he himself ties the knot
in what Audubon calls the "love-season." Audubon sets him
     in an old hat
remarkably free of lice and nits
and has him hit

high note after high note by way of exuberant meet and greet,
much as Dr. Hook and the Medicine Show touted
     themselves as a "tonic
for the soul" as far back as 1968. I'll need an 80-grit
sander belt if I'm ever to loosen the tongue

of that floorboard on the porch. The big question has to do
     with Sevin 5%,
whether I should ignore the egg-sac theory and spurt
some into the nest. I suspect one of Robert P. Lowell's
     ocean-floor vents
might summon, if not the Great Spirit, the spirit

of Tamanend, Tamanend who stalks
the Irish Catskills in search of a riddle, a rattle, a horse-coiffed
    False Face,
anything that might serve as Jenny Wren's nesting box.
The fact that I've always run two tape reels slightly out of phase

will only partly explain my engagement with the non sequitur
and the leap of the imagination (Gas! GAS!),
as I passed signs on the thruway for Woodstock and Saugerties.
I'm pretty sure Francis Scott Key's

still turning in his grave after Jimi's interwoven
shreds of his "Banner," soot, spit,
the sound hole of Richie Havens's guitar, a hubcap from
    Hubcap Heaven,
an abandoned hive, a boot, a roundabout, "the pot

that washes itself," a tin pail, a cow's skull,
a hangman's bone-and-feather lei.
Even as I set out for the Agway in Cobleskill
to replenish my supply of Sevin dust that's run so perilously low

I realize that "Walking the Steel: From Girder to Ground Zero"
closed a year ago, maybe five or fifty years back,
even as my own boy-self was clinging to the scaffolding and the
    impresario,
Bill Graham, jeuked behind the Marshall stack.

3

Then as now, the trick was to accept that a mindful rallying of
the unruly
on an eternally nameless "path"
is no less a hen's errand than proving a house wren avails of
time-release
nit-eating spiders. I'd been thinking our new beehive-

shaped sauna, or *hanjeungmak*, would be the first in the
Mohawk Valley
when it occurred to me that Korean
monks were far from being the only ones to use sweat-lodges
or flay
their guests by going against their grain

with a fifteenth-century sanding belt. The word Ojibwa itself
means "pucker"
and almost certainly refers to that half-harried, half-homesick
look on a torture victim's face. Just as, at the Black Cat Café
and Bakery,
Tony Daou offers "Thanksgiving sandwiches" all year round,
so wren-music

offers druids a permanent link between
this world and the one nearby. Some hold the "pucker" refers
to a fold

or seam in a Huron moccasin. A seamlessly served poutine
is a highlight at the American Hotel. Those Quebeckers
    learned to exfoliate

a beaver only around the time the clippers
were running opium from England to China. When it comes
    to a bridge
between epic and lyric, Stesichorus of Calabria
may have written the book, but in the matter of eating Korean
    porridge,

or *jook*, the house wren ever punches above its weight
as it pursues its interest in iron-carbon.
While I drove home last night after seeing Deep Purple at
    Bethel Woods
it came to me in a flash that the Proto-Indo-European

dherghen lies behind both the Irish *droighnean* and the
    "thorn"
in the Blackthorne Resort in East Durham. All I can do is
    sound the lyre,
however feebly, against the drone.
We've forgotten how the Troggs put out "Strange Movies" and
    "I'm on Fire"

the same year their studio meltdown
was made public. Among the poets who are closest to my heart

these days are Stesichorus and John Skelton,
poets who may dart

like Tinker Bell between the capriciousness of "Gyb, I say,
   our cat"
and the capacity to suffer
a loss greater than even Philip Sparrow. Thomas Merton's
   call to serve God
came to him in a vision at the Church of Saint Francis Xavier

on Sixteenth between Fifth and Sixth. Now Tamanend
   reports "a small mirror held
in the hand offstage and reflecting a lamp" had Tinker Bell
   flit like a ghost
from wing to wing of the Duke of York's. This allowed
the "Miss Jenny Wren" listed in the cast

to be bodied out in the mind, a house wren in his top hat,
   white tie, and tails
finding new ways with grass, weeds, hair, fur, bones, feathers,
a leaf from Owen's *Complete Poems*, running up and down
   the scale
out of a combination of euphoria

and the urge to totally eclipse
all pretenders to his throne. "Mine," he insists. "All mine."

That common spink, designated by Linnaeus as *Fringilla*
    coelebs
on account of the habits of a European chaffinch thought of,
    in the main,

as "monkish," is also given to staking out his territory
purely by means of song. That cluck's the cluck
of the match Hendrix, having covered "Wild Thing" at
    Monterey,
used to immolate his Strat. A wren's "winding down of a
    ticking clock"

in a crocodile's belly beat time for Stesichorus, Stesichorus
who once stood between two war-bands
and enthralled them with a poem. A 60-grit sanding belt is
    far too coarse,
a 120 too fine. I'm tempted to mosey over to Stewart's for a
    pint

of their signature "Crumbs
Along the Mohawk,"
an award-winning chocolate-and-graham-cracker ice cream,
seeing how they're out of 80-grit sanding belts at the
    Cobleskill Agway.

Acknowledgments

Acknowledgments are due to the editors of the following publications, in which versions of some of these poems first appeared: *American Journal of Irish Studies*, *Belfast Telegraph*, *Blackbox Manifold*, *Harvard Review*, *The Irish Times*, *London Review of Books*, *The Nation*, *The New York Review of Books*, *The New York Times*, *The New York Times Style Magazine*, *The New Yorker*, *Ploughshares*, *PN Review*, *Poem-a-Day* (Academy of American Poets), *Poetry Ireland Review*, *The Sewanee Review*, *Stand*, *The Times Literary Supplement*, *The Village Voice*, and *Winter Pages*.

"The Great Horse of the World" was printed as a broadside in 2016 by the Virginia Arts of the Book Center. A limited edition of *"Encheiresin Naturae*," with engravings by Barry Moser, was published by the Nawakum Press in 2015. Section 2 of "Memphis" was included in *WB Yeats 150/2015*, published by Sears O'Riordan Fine Art Editions, Dublin. "Belfast Hymn" was commissioned by the Grand Central Hotel in Belfast. "1916: The Eoghan Rua Variations" was commissioned by New York University as part of the university's celebration of the centenary of the Irish Rising. "July 1, 1916: With the Ulster Division" was commissioned by the National Centre for Writing. These last two were included in *Rising to the Rising*, which was published by Gallery Press in 2016. "Wilfred Owen: November 4, 1918" appeared in *Peace Poetry*, a pamphlet published in 2018 by the Royal Society of Literature. "Armistice Day" was included in *Armistice: A Laureate's Choice of Poems of War and Peace*, edited by Carol Ann Duffy and published by Faber & Faber in 2018. "Edward Elgar: Cello Concerto in E Minor (1919)" was included in *Ways of Hearing*, published in 2019 by Princeton University Press. "At Tuam" was commissioned by *The New York Times*, in which it appeared, and was also published as a postcard by Poetry Ireland in 2018. "Likely to Go Unnoticed" was published in a limited edition by the Graphic Studio Dublin in 2017. "April in New Hope" appeared in *Berryman's Fate*, published by Arlen House in 2014. "The Door" appeared in *Looking at the Stars: An Anthology of Irish Writing in Aid of the Dublin Simon Community*, published in 2016 by the Munster Literature Centre. "Aubade" was included in *The Best American Poetry 2019*, edited by Major Jackson and published by Scribner Poetry. "Superior Aloeswood" appeared in *Resistance, Rebellion, Life: 50 Poems Now*, published in 2017 by Alfred A. Knopf. "At the River" appeared in *Long Walk Home: Reflections on Bruce Springsteen*, published by Rutgers University Press in 2019. "Putsch" appeared in *Eavan Boland: Inside History*, published by Arlen House in 2016. Section 1 of "Frolic and Detour" appeared in *The Eloquent Poem*, published in 2019 by Persea Books. Several of these poems appeared in *Superior Aloeswood*, an interim collection published by Enitharmon in 2017.